Doctor Nicole Audet

The Magic of Empathy

Theory and Practice

Foreword by Ruth Vachon
President and CEO of the Quebec
Business Women's Network

RFAQ

Réseau des Femmes
d'affaires du Québec

Dr. Nicole PUBLISHING

© 2019 Doctor Nicole Audet for Dr. Nicole Publishing
All rights reserved
Legal deposit trimester 2019
Bibliothèque et Archives nationales du Québec
Library and Archives Canada

ISBN (Soft cover) 978-1-989041-89-5
ISBN (Hard cover) 978-1-989041-94-9
ISBN (MOBI) 978-1-989041-91-8
ISBN (PDF) 978-1-989041-90-1
ISBN (EPUB) 978-1-989041-92-5
ISBN (Audiobook) 978-1-989041-93-2

This book is available in French with the title:
La Magie de l'empathie (Théorie et pratique)
ISBN 978-1-989041-83-3

Photograph of the author: Emmanuèle Garnier,
Le Médecin du Québec
Graphic Design: Italique
Publisher: Dr. Nicole Publishing
Author: Dr. Nicole Audet
Book Editing: Katrina Baldassarre and Carol Thompson
Proofreading: Carol Thompson
Translation: Gotranscript gotranscript.com
Cover Page Illustration Credit: AdobeStock (Aliaksandra)
Inner Pages Illustrations Credits: AdobeStock
    (p. 12 : BadBrother, p. 46 : ZYTA.eM, p. 84 : lembergvector)

Websites: DrNicoleBook.com and NicoleAudet.com (French)

The content of this book may not be reproduced or shared without
the written permission of the author and publisher, Dr. Nicole
Publishing.

The author is available to speak at conferences or book signing on
the subject of empathic communication. Please contact the author
at: nicole@nicoleaudet.com.

The author of this book invites you to write a review on e-book
distributor websites.

Two stories included in this book, "Amy's Tears" and "Witness of
Last Breath," have been published in the book *Bouillon de poulet
pour l'âme des Québécois,* Béliveau Éditeur, 2012.

Who Is This Book For?

The *Magic of Empathy* demystifies the key concepts in communication and illustrates them with examples. It is intended for the general public, particularly those interested in learning about empathic communication.

To differentiate my book from other books on the subject of communication, I devoted almost half of my book to telling stories that have improved my life, both as a mother and as a doctor. I hope that you will be surprised and touched as I was by the outcome of these empathic and magical conversations.

THIS BOOK SHOULD NOT BE USED AS A SUBSTITUTE FOR THERAPY, WHERE PROFESSIONAL INTERVENTION IS REQUIRED. IF YOU REQUIRE THE SERVICES OF A HEALTH PROFESSIONAL, DO NOT HESITATE TO CONTACT ONE. THIS BOOK DOES NOT PROVIDE TOOLS TO NEUTRALIZE COMMUNICATIONS WITH AGGRESSIVE, ABUSIVE, OR MANIPULATIVE INDIVIDUALS. THE AUTHOR AND PUBLISHER ARE NOT RESPONSIBLE FOR ANY MISINTERPRETATION OF THE CONTENTS OF THIS BOOK.

Table of Contents

5

Quotes

"*If you're talking, you're not listening.*"
—Buddha

"*Most people do not listen
with the intent to understand;
they listen with the intent to reply.*"
—Stephen R. Covey

"*We have two ears and one mouth
so that we can listen twice as much
as we speak.*"
—Zeno of Citium

"*Talking is a necessity,
listening is an art.*"
—Goethe

"*When I listen to people talk, all I hear
is what they're not telling me.*"
—Bob Dylan

Foreword

RUTH VACHON, President and CEO of the Quebec Business Women's Network

I n both our private and professional lives, time slips through our fingers. As our children grow older, our parents and friends age as well. The emergence of social media as our main source for information has caused us to seek out less and less meaningful interactions. These new methods of exchanging information have resulted in our losing the ability to listen to others. It's about time we changed this, now more than ever.

The other day, I was speaking to an acquaintance. Her life was in absolute shambles. Over the course of a single summer, she lost her husband to cancer, her mother passed away and her dog ran away, all while worrying about her children. She came over to my house as I was working on a time-sensitive task. My first instinct was to cut our conversation short. I ended up listening to her speak for over an hour.

From one question to the next, after many tears were shed, I became painfully aware of the struggles and challenges that plagued her every day. As she was leaving, she turned and said to me, "You're so kind. Thank you for taking the time to listen to me. I have an entirely new perspective now. Our conversation took a huge weight off my shoulders. You can't even imagine!"

As much as this conversation was beneficial to her, it was also a learning opportunity for me. Since that moment, I became a better listener to those around me. Even when life feels like it's passing by me, I must remain vigilant, looking out for those who need me, and, above all, keep my heart "open" to others. Despite the hustle and bustle of daily life, I want to take the time to interact sincerely with others and enjoy these fleeting, precious moments.

In *The Magic of Empathy,* Dr. Nicole Audet, a faithful member of the Quebec Business Women's Network, gives us the tools to practice authentic speech and empathic listening. Thank you, Nicole, for enriching our daily lives one conversation at a time.

Acknowledgements

To my husband Sylvain Boulanger and my literary agent Danielle Hampson: thank you for your support and feedback, which have helped improve the quality of this book.

To Elizabeth Triassi: thank you for encouraging me to write on this topic.

To Ruth Vachon, President and CEO of Reseau des Femmes D'Affaires du Quebec (Quebec Business Women's Network): thank you very much for writing the foreword.

9

Empathy is a choice.

Introduction

vividly remember the day I had to pass my medical school admissions interview, with a few valuable minutes to convince my interviewer that I deserved a place in the university's most coveted faculty.

To achieve my goal, I began preparing months in advance. I studied the curriculum, asked students what questions I would be asked, and practiced with my father. He told me to visualize my success and to get a good night's sleep the night before the interview. His wise words are forever engraved in my memory: "When all skills are equal, only positive attitudes can make a difference."

I arrived at the interview well-dressed, calm, and smiling. Thanks to my research, I remembered that the doctor who was interviewing me was the first woman to have a degree from a medical school in Quebec. I sat there in silence and complete and utter admiration for the woman before me. I wanted to be just like her. I was in the presence of my idol. Looking back, I think she could tell I was star-struck. I felt listened to and respected throughout the interview.

The fifteen-minute interview went exactly as I had planned. I can't remember anything we actually said to each other. However, I can close my eyes and still feel the magic of that moment, a moment that has changed the course of my life. A few weeks later, I received a letter in the mail offering me a place in their medical school. I was so happy! Fate nonetheless intervened, and I ended up accepting a position at a competing university.

More than forty years have passed since that interview when I felt vulnerable exposing myself to my inteviewer. Today, I know that I succeeded because I spoke from the heart. I planned my interview by choosing the right words to make myself understood. Since then, I have had thousands of opportunities to improve my empathic communication skills, both in speaking and in listening. I must confess that the learning process was long and difficult, but thanks to my perseverance, I can testify today that these skills have helped me to get to know myself better and to make myself better equipped to help others.

Now I want to reveal the secrets and magic of empathic interpersonal communication. Speaking to be understood and listening to understand are two skills that have the power to change the life of anyone who possesses them. To enrich our conversations with empathy, we must recognize the other person's emotions, receive them without judgement, and help them evolve so that they can allow us to experience an unforgettable moment. On the other hand, to attract empathy, it is necessary to speak truthfully and to accept that you will evolve as you interact with the other person. Be prepared, as during an empathic communication, anything can happen.

Putting this wonderful theory aside, becoming a doctor has been a very challenging experience with countless obstacles. I have lived through many difficult experiences, and I have chosen to bury them deep within myself, hoping to forget them. In my interactions with my patients, colleagues or family members, I did not always take the time to listen to them with empathy. Looking back, I realize that I would speak to others with the sole intention of imparting my point of view while changing everyone else's. You can imagine my frustration; I kept talking, and no one around me would change!

I was unhappy. I wanted to change the course of my life and have more fun doing my job. To achieve this, I had to be willing to do some soul-searching exercises with the help of a professional. I had to learn how to communicate to be understood. That is how I got through my ever-mounting obstacles, one at a time, so that I could move forward.

Finally, I developed my empathic listening skills. I can confidently say that ever since then, my life has changed for the better. I think I've been able to help many of my patients and other people I have encountered to better understand each other and to act in ways that enriched the lives of all those involved.

As I refined my new skills, I had some successes and some failures, which I will share with you in the second part of this book. However, I will be the first to admit that I am not always taking my own advice. I've had times where I was busy, overwhelmed, or just in a hurry, and I would meet with patients without taking the time to truly listen to them. They would leave my office frustrated, and some even filed complaints against me. I always came up with excuses to justify myself, but deep down, I knew that the quality of my communication had been poor and that I was to blame.

I occasionally felt ignored by my bosses, my colleagues, and suppliers. I finally came to the conclusion that I needed professional help to better understand myself and to build my self-esteem. I had to find my voice, a voice that would set me apart as a family doctor. After many sessions with my therapists, I felt great. I knew that self-improvement would require a lot of introspection. Despite the daunting nature of this task, I had a lot of fun doing it.

It is quite easy to find books, speeches, or websites about empathic listening. However, it is difficult to find resources to help you to learn how to speak from your heart and to be understood. My book tries to fill this void.

It is worth wondering why it is so rare to meet people who have the ability to confide in others as well as listen. Try to remember a time in your life when speaking from your heart would have been good for you. Don't you have a little inner voice stopping you from speaking for fear of being judged by others? Prejudice, lack of money, or lack of resources prevent many people from confiding in professionals, or even in loved ones.

Let's examine another factor responsible for the evolution of communication that has led to the isolation of individuals. Most people are familiar with the technology that has radically changed how we communicate. To illustrate my point, imagine that you are in the early 1970s. No one had a cell phone, a few lucky ones had a Walkman with headphones, and only the wealthy had color televisions. Families ate meals together, often with a large number of people around the table. It sometimes would become quite loud, but everyone would be talking to each other.

Nowadays, new technologies have invaded our daily lives. Even elementary school children own cell phones, communicate via Facebook and Snapchat, and spend hours playing video games that are sometimes quite violent.

Isolation is also a growing problem. Studies show that single people occupy up to half of the dwellings in some cities, creating serious isolation problems. These changes impact the quality of communication between people and within families.

I have written this book for all who want to get back to the basics and unlock the secrets of enriched communication in the context of a conversation between two people. Using scientific data, examples, references and exercises, you will learn to speak to be understood, to listen to understand, and to do it with authenticity and sincerity. These basic skills will positively influence the course of your life, as well as those of your loved ones or your professional circle. It is quite magical!

OVER THE YEARS, I HAVE COME TO LEARN THAT SPEAKING AND LISTENING WITH ONE'S HEART ARE THE TWO FUNDAMENTAL SKILLS OF PEOPLE WHO POSITIVELY INFLUENCE THOSE AROUND THEM.

In Theory

First and foremost, it is important to define the concept of empathy and sympathy to appreciate the science of authentic communication.

Empathy and Sympathy

To avoid confusion, let's first clearly define the concepts of empathy and sympathy, as you must be able to distinguish between these two basic concepts.

During empathic communication, listening should be active, positive, and without judgment or attempts to influence the other person's ideas. Manipulation has no place in empathic communication.

The empathic communicator can recognize the emotions of their interlocutors, name them, welcome them, and allow them to progress for the sake of their interlocutors. In other words, empathic communicators can put themselves in another person's shoes and listen to them without losing their own identity or be forced to approve of the content of their interlocutors' ideas. Empathic communicators can be seen as catalysts that help others to find a solution to their problems.

Sympathy, on the other hand, implies a fusion of emotions. In addition to recognizing another person's emotions, you feel them as well. This fusion does not help them progress toward solving their problems. Certainly, they will feel supported; however, sympathy may devolve into pity, which can be useless or even harmful.

Empathic communication is based on emotions, which progress throughout the conversation. Communicators work in stages. First, they focus on detecting emotions. Once they feel these emotions, they must identify them (joy, anger, disappointment, etc.). Once these first steps are completed, communicators start their investigation to understand the underlying motivations of their interlocutors. To achieve this, it is critical that communicators ask open-ended questions and let the interlocutors express themselves freely to uncover the latter's motivations. Obviously, this step must be without judgment, abuse of power, or manipulation. Finally, empathic communicators will be able to help their interlocutors do the work to evolve and transform their emotions. For example, when dealing with good communicators, angry individuals can transform their negative emotions and thoughts into more peaceful ones and can even come up with creative ways to solve their problems. Figure 1 illustrates the pathway to manage emotions during an empathic conversation.

**SYMPATHY COMFORTS.
EMPATHY MAKES ONE EVOLVE.**

Figure 1 *Emotions during an empathic conversation*

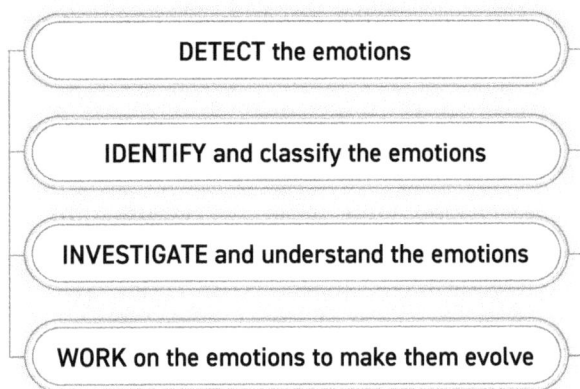

DETECT the emotions

IDENTIFY and classify the emotions

INVESTIGATE and understand the emotions

WORK on the emotions to make them evolve

19

___

WARNING

___

If you have real or perceived power or authority
over your interlocutors (that is, you are a parent,
boss, or teacher), be extra careful in your efforts
to communicate empathetically. Whether you like it
or not, your position will influence the course of the
conversation. It is enough to be aware of it, and not try
to deny or ignore it.

___

Emotions

One of the tasks of the empathic communicator is to detect, identify, and understand emotions.

Table 1 provides a list of emotions classified into two categories, labeled *positive* and *negative*. Personally, I find this classification quite arbitrary because throughout a conversation, it is common to experience a range of emotions. I think it would be more fitting to classify this list into *happy emotions* and *emotions to work on.*

Well-channeled anger can lead you to experience emotions that ultimately allow you to solve a problem. For example, during a period of grief, the denial that one experiences before feeling angry often gives way to recovery.

Emotions are like infectious diseases; they are highly contagious. Don't believe me? Just watch a funny movie with your family, and in a few minutes, everyone will be laughing wholeheartedly, no matter how difficult their day might have been. On the other hand, imagine a brother-in-law who gets angry at a family meal; you will surely agree that the general mood of the room will be subdued as a result. Some will accuse him of ruining dinner. With your new knowledge of empathic communication, keep smiling. You can put your interlocutors at ease and keep the conversation flowing.

I've always given my patients some tips to learn how to manage their emotions. To avoid reacting too quickly, I first advise them to pause and welcome their anger by telling themselves, "I know you want me to explode, but I refuse to do it now. Let's make an appointment for tonight, and we'll solve our problems together." Patients who adopt this habit improve their communication skills. Second, I advise them to write in an emotional journal regularly. Writing is a powerful therapeutic tool.

Table 1 *The Emotions*

Happy Emotions	Emotions to Work On
Amusement	Anger
Confidence	Denial
Enjoyment	Despair
Enthusiasm	Disgust
Euphoria	Envy
Gratitude	Fear
Hope	Hate
Joy	Negative Surprise
Love	Sadness
Serenity	Shame

Before going further, remember these two important features about emotions.

> **EMOTIONS ARE EXPERIENCED WITH THE HEART AND MANAGED WITH THE MIND.**

> **EMOTIONS ARE AS CONTAGIOUS AS THE FLU.**

Talking versus Listening

Did you know that our speech rate is one of the most important factors that influence the ability of an average person to understand us?

Let's look at some examples:

1. The average speed of standard speech is about 150 words per minute.

2. Experienced communicators will speak more slowly. If they have a speech rate between 120 to 140 words per minute and choose short phrases using a simplified and colloquial vocabulary while clearly repeating their main message, they considerably increase their chances of being understood.

22

   Let's use President Barack Obama's famous keynote speech as an example. His three words

   ## "Yes, we can"

   are still in the minds of all his admirers. For more proof, just analyze his speeches. He speaks slowly, uses a simple vocabulary that can be understood by everyone, and has mastered the art of silence and pauses, which have the effect of reinforcing the message he is conveying. This charismatic former president repeated his unique message at least six or seven times in speeches that did not need to that long. In contrast, The ex-French President Jacques Chirac spoke at a very slow rate of one hundred words per minute. At this rate, the audience might fall asleep.

3. At the other extreme of the spectrum, radio journalists can speak up to 230 words per minute, due to time

constraints. This rate reduces their ability to be well understood by everyone unless their subject really captivates listeners.

Communication only works when one person is talking and a second person is listening. We have seen that the first person must speak at a certain rate for the listener to be understood by the speaker. But what about the person who is listening?

Evidence suggests that the average human brain can accurately interpret more than 500 words per minute in a person's dominant language. The unconscious part of your brain can process nearly 250 words per minute, filling in the gaps between what someone is telling you and what you understand. With such fast speech processing, it is not surprising that listeners can become easily distracted or fall asleep unless the subject or content of the conversation truly captivates them. Consequently, without any real intention of listening and focus, individuals listen with the intent to respond, preparing their responses as their interlocutor is speaking. Imagine a couple bickering. There can be no dialogue; there are only two people speaking at the same time without any form of listening.

23

These simple facts reveal why it is so complex to speak to be understood and to listen to understand. To succeed in our endeavor, we must practice, analyze our failures, and start over again.

To reach the level of depth necessary to qualify a communication as empathic, it requires commitment, authenticity, and a real desire to positively improve the relationship. This type of communication usually involves a great deal of emotional intensity from the people involved.

Hearing versus Listening

In Table 2, the difference between hearing and listening is explained. For a sound to be heard, it must vibrate the small bones (ossicles) behind the eardrums and then travel along the auditory nerve to an area of the brain that perceives the sound. To be interpreted or understood, the sound must be decoded. For example, if you hear tourists speaking in a language you don't know, you hear them; however, you do not understand them because you do not know the correct code to interpret the sounds you hear.

Table 2 *Hearing versus Listening*

Hearing	Listening
Involuntary	Voluntary
Sounds travel to the brain through the nervous system	Sounds travel to the brain through the nervous system
Brain is stimulated	Brain interprets, gives meaning
You hear	You understand

To illustrate this concept, let's use the example of the telephone game. In this game, the first player whispers a sentence in his neighbor's ear. The latter whispers to their neighbor what they had heard and so on until the last player repeats out loud what they understood. The more players there are, the greater the discrepancy between the first and final sentence. A distortion of the original message occurs. However, each player is certain that they have repeated what they heard.

In this game, despite a real desire to listen, the message still gets distorted from one individual to another.

The outcome of this game should convince us all that conveying a message and listening to a message are complex tasks that require high-level skills. The good news is that with commitment, these skills can be acquired.

Later in this book, we will learn how to put these theories into practice.

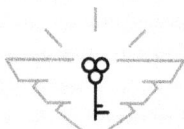

WHAT TO REMEMBER FROM THE THEORY

1

Learn to recognize the other person's emotions,
name them, receive them, and make them evolve
to help the other person solve their problem.

2

You need commitment, authenticity,
and a real desire to positively improve
the relationship in order to reach the level of depth
required to qualify a communication as empathic.

3

Remember that the feeling of empathy
infers a great deal of emotional intensity
on those involved. Be prepared to go through
these moments in total humility.

In Practice

After reviewing the theory of empathic communication, let's see how to become empathic communicators. In this section, you will learn how to speak and listen with your heart.

Speaking to Be Understood

There are times when we need to communicate a message. Let's take a few examples from our daily lives:

- ☞ You want to convince your parents to get on board with your plans after high school.

- ☞ You meet with your employer to discuss your salary.

- ☞ You want to discuss a disagreement with a colleague.

- ☞ You want to convince your spouse that you need to save more money.

- ☞ You want to negotiate new rates with a supplier.

All these situations have one thing in common: a sensitive subject that needs to be communicated to a parent, colleague, boss, spouse, or supplier. These are not ordinary conversations that require no preparation. To succeed in their goals, these individuals must prepare themselves, select the right arguments, and promote their ideas without insulting or humiliating the people to whom they are speaking.

The first thing to know is that a relationship is dynamic and therefore subject to change. Before the meeting, if possible, do a positive visualization session. Imagine all the steps of the meeting, from beginning to end, just as an athlete at the Olympics visualizes winning the gold medal.

An effective and empathic relationship must be nurtured, cherished, and loved. The success of an emphatic conversation lies in its authenticity. True and heartfelt communication is key.

To get ready for a meeting, do the suggested exercises at the end of this book.

28

Listening to Understand

"Talking is good but keeping quiet is better."
—Jean de La Fontaine (*The Bear and the Garden Lover*)

Let's imagine again the situations mentioned above, but this time, you are the one who has to listen to understand.

🗩 Your son wants to explain his post-secondary education plans to you.

🗩 Your employee is talking to you about his salary.

🗩 Your colleague is telling you that she does not agree with your point of view.

✍ Your spouse wants to change the family budget to increase the amount you save.

✍ Your business partner wants to renegotiate your prices.

The same advice applies to communicators who are listening, with some adjustments. Remember that you are in a relationship with someone who wants to talk to you. Like your interlocutors, you want the relationship to be dynamic, authentic, and pleasant. Open your heart to reduce the risk of conflict. You will be surprised by the results.

To get ready for your meeting, complete the exercises at the end of this book.

29

Open- or Closed-Ended Questions

There are two types of questions: close-ended and open-ended. The first type, close-ended questions, require short and succinct answers, often "yes" or "no." They are sometimes useful to quickly steer a conversation in one direction or another.

The second type, open-ended questions, allows the other person to formulate a more complete response. Ideally, your questions should be free from any judgment. I suggest using as many open-ended questions as possible during your empathic conversations.

Table 3 provides some examples of open- and closed-ended questions that people might ask you during a job interview, an assessment, or negotiation.

Table 3 *A comparison of open-ended and closed-ended questions*

Open-ended questions	Close-ended questions
How are you feeling?	Are you happy today?
What are your expectations?	Do you have expectations?
In what ways are you satisfied with our meeting?	Are you satisfied with our meeting?
What could be done to resolve this conflict in a way that would satisfy everyone?	Is it possible to solve this conflict in a way that would satisfy everyone?

Successful Responses

During a conversation, everyone takes turns asking or answering questions, much like a game of tennis. You hit the ball and receive it without knowing how it will come back to you. A smash can happen so fast! Be ready and well prepared.

Remember that some answers are more inviting than others and will encourage your interlocutor to continue the dialogue.

For example, if you say, "I hear what you're saying," you are showing respect without necessarily agreeing with the content of other person's speech. The door remains open to discussing your point of view.

You might also say, "I would like to know why you think that way." Isn't this a good example of how you can encourage the person to whom you are talking to proceed? Or you could say, "If I understood correctly, what you're telling me is that..." and then rephrase what you understood. The other person will be happy to confirm or correct your understanding before the conversation continues.

Staying calm allows you to neutralize potentially explosive situations. I can remember an aggressive customer on the phone. I patiently listened to him before answering, saying, "If I were you, I would be angry too, but if you don't mind, I'd like to share my viewpoint with you."

He immediately calmed down and listened. We spoke calmly, and our conversation ended on a friendly note, even though the problem was still unresolved. The client knew I would take care of his problems, and that I would keep him informed. I kept my promise.

31

Here's a good trick if you work in customer service over the phone. Have a mirror nearby. Always smile. The customer will feel your emotion even without seeing you.

To be successful in your responses, avoid responding by saying, "Yes, but..." If you use this phrase, your interlocutors may think that you were preparing your answer while they were talking—and that you weren't listening to them. The other common phrase you should avoid using in your responses is "Listen to me carefully..." This phrase will close many doors because it means "I am right, and you are not."

Non-Verbal Language

"The most important thing in communication is to listen to what the other person is not saying."
—Peter Drucker

I could write a book, even an encyclopedia, on the importance of non-verbal language (synergology) in communication. Almost half of communication is non-verbal, which is why it is so vital.

Here are some elements of non-verbal language that are useful in reassuring your interlocutors when you are engaging in empathic communication.

✍ Firmly shake their hand.

✍ Maintain eye contact without staring.

✍ Smile with conviction.

- Control the volume, rate, and timbre of your voice.

- Dress properly for the occasion; remember that even the colors you wear influence communication.

- Maintain an appropriate physical distance between you and your interlocutor. Close proximity like that between spouses (intimate distance) can become inappropriate in other circumstances (social or public distance) where it is more appropriate to keep a certain distance between you and your interlocutor.

- Try to keep your arms open throughout the conversation. Keeping arms crossed or closed is not appropriate during an empathic conversation.

- Watch your body odors (breath, sweat, smoke) which can inconvenience the person to whom you are speaking.

33

Practice doing the right things at the right time during simple conversations and analyze your performance to improve the quality of your empathetic communication and your emotional intelligence.

THE BEST WAY TO IMPROVE YOUR NON-VERBAL
COMMUNICATION SKILLS IS TO FILM YOURSELF
DURING A SIMULATED INTERVIEW AND ANALYZE
THE VIDEO WITH A COMMUNICATION EXPERT.

The Power of Silence

**"We often repent for talking,
never for keeping quiet."**
—Plutarch

34

**"Learn to be silent.
Let your quiet mind listen and absorb."**
—Pythagoras

The most valuable tool available to empathetic communicators is silence. During a pause, people have ample time
to feel an emotion, to look for elements of an answer in
their mind, and to prepare the best possible response
strategy. If you ask several questions in a row during a
discussion, you will only get answers to the last questions,
making the first questions completely useless. In addition,
you might exhaust your interlocutor, who will verbally or
non-verbally express their desire to end the conversation.

If you want to become a communicator who is highly appreciated for their empathetic abilities, learn to respect silence. Always pause for at least five seconds after asking an open-ended question. I guarantee that you will be amazed by the results.

Use this pause to adopt a calm and inviting non-verbal posture. For example, maintain eye contact without staring, keep your arms open, and smile while leaning slightly toward the person to whom you are listening.

35

I don't know if this is a coincidence,
but the word **"listen"** contains the same letters
as the word **"silent."**

Recipe for Guaranteed Failure

Having an empathic communication is always difficult. Here is a list of actions to avoid if you want to increase your chances of successful communication.

- Choosing a bad time to meet.

- Not preparing before the meeting.

- Raising your voice.

- Asking several questions in a row.

- Breaking any silence as soon as it occurs.

- Disrespecting your interlocutors.

- Humiliating or denigrating your interlocutors.

- Wanting to win at all costs.

- Manipulating your interlocutors.

You can imagine the consequences of employing any of the above actions. It is always best to postpone a complex and emotional conversation if you are struggling to control your emotions. Once the relationship is broken or torn apart, you will need substantial energy to restore it and will then have to start all over again to achieve your initial goals.

Talking with a Child

Communication with young children requires special attention and care. Most children under eight or nine years old are unable to understand complex expressions. To illustrate this, I will share with you the story of a visit I made to kindergarten and first grade children.

The teacher had invited me to present my book, *The Magic of the Human Body*, from the Felix and Booboo picture-books series. In this book, I added expressions about the human body. For example:

- To have a heavy heart.

- Catch someone's eye.

- To put your foot in your mouth.

- Pain in the neck.

- To be a birdbrain.

37

The teachers and I had a lot of fun listening to the meanings the children attributed to these expressions. None of the children understood them. They all became anxious thinking that somebody could catch their eye. When I asked them what they would do if they were a birdbrain, two students quickly raised their hands. The first one told me that he could finally eat earthworms, the second one that he would fly over his house.

This story illustrates the importance of adjusting your vocabulary to your interlocutor's ability to understand, especially with children. Don't be surprised if your child refuses to go out if you say, "It's raining cats and dogs."

The importance of adjusting your vocabulary also applies when there is a knowledge gap between you and your interlocutor (for example, doctor and patient, lawyer and client, engineer and client). A patient once told me that the suppositories I prescribed had cured him, but they had an unpleasant taste.

If you are proficient at using specialized vocabulary and are talking to children, make sure to adjust your language accordingly to establish that you're properly understood.

Handling a Toxic Conversation

Readers have told me, "Sometimes you need to put an end to a toxic relationship." I replied that they were absolutely right. If you have a relationship with a manipulative and/or abusive person, the situation becomes completely different. It is better to end the relationship, with as much respect as possible, with those who have no intention of listening to you. There are several books and websites

available where you can learn how to recognize manipu-
lators and toxic relationships. The purpose of my book is
to get you ready to communicate with people of good will.

However, these clues will help you recognize a toxic
conversation:

🖐 The time of the meeting is imposed and non-negotiable.

🖐 The meeting is improvised.

🖐 You sense contempt, are being accused of something,
or are receiving thinly veiled threats.

🖐 You are being bombarded with questions and don't
have time to answer.

🖐 Your interlocutor does not listen to you, interrupts
you, or can't stand silence.

🖐 Your interlocutor is trying to humiliate you.

🖐 You feel that your chances of progressing with your
interlocutor are nil. Your opponent is only interested
in winning points in their favor.

🖐 You sense an abuse of power that is difficult to
circumvent.

If you are ever caught up in a discussion like this, I
recommend that you put an end to it by clearly stating
your discomfort.

Here are some examples of statements I have used
successfully with manipulative people:

- "Right now, I don't feel comfortable continuing this conversation. It's better to meet again when we have both calmed down. I think it will take us at least twenty-four hours to get there."

- "Right now, I don't appreciate the tone you're using. I suggest you change it or we make an appointment to finish our discussion."

In the second case, if the person sincerely apologizes and changes their tone, resume the conversation.

In these two examples, I choose to start with the words "Right now" to reposition the person in time. From experience, I have learned that an abusive person either lives in the past or in the future, but has difficulties living in the present. I use a calm tone and speak in a low voice to smooth things over. Then I state my discomfort, which cannot be negotiated or argued. I conclude by suggesting a second meeting. With this offer, everyone gets a second chance. Nobody deserves a life sentence for yelling once. After all, everyone has their moments where they aren't at their best.

This approach is successful in most cases. During the second meeting, your interlocutor will often apologize and will be happy to be forgiven. Your relationship stands a good chance of evolving. This technique is particularly helpful with teenagers who have trouble controlling their emotions. Putting an end to a manipulative conversation can be a good lesson for those who are trying to abuse your trust. It is then up to them to do their own self-examination to improve themselves.

Unfortunately, despite all your goodwill, nothing can fix a toxic relationship based on domination and psychological harassment a relationship that is only aimed at destroying you. Under these circumstances, the relationship must be terminated for you to thrive.

Creative Communication

In my experience, empathic communication can go far beyond trying to understand, comfort, or welcome the other person. In some cases, when two individuals are talking with the real intention of solving a problem, communication reaches a higher level, which I call *creative communication.*

Imagine two people faced with a problem and negotiating to find a win-win solution. The story "Mom, I Am Planning a Sleepover at My Friend's House," shared later in this book (p. 51), is a good example of creative communication.

41

High-level creative communication requires a good deal of humility for those involved in solving the problem. To achieve this, it is better to be well prepared and to be really committed to finding a solution.

Ideally, to become an empathic communicator, choose the best possible time for both parties involved, get prepared, stay focused on your objectives, respect pauses, and be respectful.

42

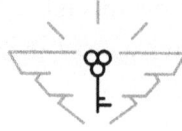

WHAT TO REMEMBER FROM THE PRACTICE

1

Take care of your relationships; they need to be nourished, loved, and nurtured.

2

Ask open-ended questions and answer effectively to enhance your conversation with your interlocutors.

3

Silently count to five after each question and after each answer.
This will increase your empathic communication skills.

———

4

Learn how to interpret non-verbal
language and how to respond appropriately
in accordance with the message
you want to convey.

5

Identify toxic conversations,
defuse them, or stop them
if they cannot be recovered.

6

Remain open and humble;
find creative solutions to your problems
by communicating with others.

7

Adjust your vocabulary according
to your interlocutor's ability
to understand.

———

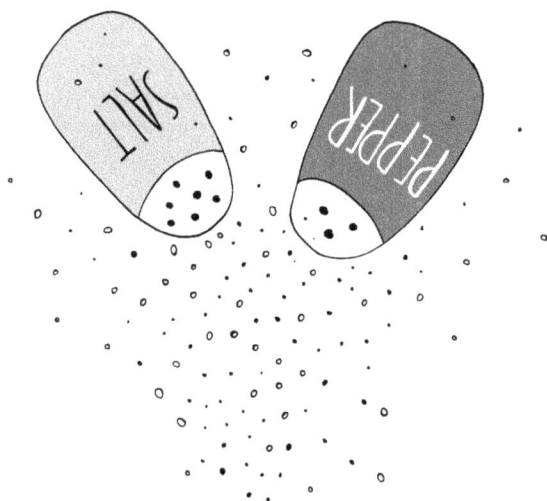

Add empathy
to your conversations,
it is delicious!

For Practice: Exercises

To make the most out of this book section, I recommend that you grab a piece of paper and a pencil and do the exercises. Writing helps to prioritize our ideas by clarifying them. The more important the communication is, the greater the need for appropriate preparation. You will practice how to get prepared to speak and listen with empathy.

Speaking to Be Understood

Imagine some real-life situations. Before a competition, performers spend countless hours rehearsing. Employers select well-prepared candidates who have made an effort to research their company's mission, vision, and values. Customers are more willing to purchase a product from a competent salesperson that can explain their products and demonstrate how they can meet their needs.

45

Before the Meeting

To become prepared, do some research, and set your goals to increase your chances to find a win-win solution to your problems.

🖉 Find out who you want to talk to and where they stand relative to you in the hierarchy.

- Is your interlocutor a relative, a friend, a colleague, a supplier, or a partner?

- Be more cautious when planning to speak to an aggressive or manipulative person.

☞ What are your expectations or objectives? Write them all down. Then, for efficiency, choose one or two from among the most important objectives. If there are too many objectives, you will probably need more than one meeting to resolve them all.

☞ Try to find the best time to ask for a meeting and make your request. For example, Monday mornings and Friday afternoons are rarely the most suitable times.

☞ Estimate the time allocated for the meeting and mention it in your invitation. Your interlocutor will perceive this as a sign of respect of their time.

☞ If you think that the meeting will be too emotional and the situation too complex, role-playing with an experienced coach may help you. This type of situation will require that you keep your emotions under control. Remember that anger will only make you lose control of your objectives during sensitive conversations.

☞ Do as much research as possible to know the needs of your interlocutors. What can you do to help him or her fulfill them? Interlocutors are more sensitive to your needs if they feel that you care about their own needs. Your chances of finding a win-win solution will be increased.

☞ Don't arrive empty-handed. Prepare documents or examples to prove your arguments. These documents will help to show your commitment.

☞ Visualize the meeting; write and practice as many open-ended questions as possible. Rewrite and refine them to make them perfect.

During the Meeting

Even if you have well-prepared objectives, be aware that anything can happen during a meeting. Stay calm, confident, and focused. Keep in mind that everybody wants win-win solutions even for very complex problems.

☞ At the beginning of the interaction, be sure to thank the person you are meeting for their time. This will help create a trusting environment suitable for the upcoming discussion.

47

☞ Quickly state the purpose of the meeting and reiterate the time you think the meeting will take.

☞ Listen to the other person's reactions.

☞ Ask each of your prepared open-ended questions, one at a time.

☞ Skillfully make use of silence and pauses by counting to five after asking a question or after answering a question. Your success is guaranteed!

☞ Ideally, conclude the meeting with two winners.

☞ Propose another meeting for a follow-up.

🖐 Before concluding, ask your interlocutor to summarize the meeting and correct any misinterpretations, if necessary.

After the Meeting

The meeting may be over, but your exercise is not. Writing a postmortem analysis will help you to improve your empathic communication skills for future use.

🖐 After the meeting, write down your impressions, and try to identify your best and worst strategies and learn from your strengths and weaknesses. This will improve your ability to speak and be understood.

🖐 Prepare the follow-up meeting with the same level of thoroughness as the initial meeting.

Listening to Understand

"Talking is a necessity, listening is an art."
—Goethe

You have received an invitation to discuss a specific topic. This request may come from a family member, an employee, a boss, or a business partner. The sooner you receive the invitation, the sooner you will be able to prepare to maximize your chances of concluding the discussion with two winners. These exercises will help you improve your empathic communication skills.

Before the Meeting

Even if you have not called the meeting, it does not mean that you should not be well prepared. If possible, do your best to follow these rules:

☞ Prepare for the meeting by writing down your weaknesses. Doing so will allow you to be more conscious of them, and you will actively work toward improving them.

☞ Negotiate the best time for the meeting. Propose several times that are suitable for you.

☞ Note in your agenda the time scheduled for the meeting.

☞ Imagine what questions you might be asked and have the answers ready.

☞ If the situation seems complex, role-playing with an experienced coach can help you prepare.

☞ If you think it is necessary that a third party attend the meeting, inform your interlocutors in advance and ask for their agreement.

☞ Find out what your interlocutor's needs are and be prepared to help them meet these.

During the Meeting

This moment is important for everyone involved. Meetings are sometimes unpredictable; be sure to stay calm, focused, and open-minded. Remember to listen carefully before speaking.

49

🖐 Make a promise to listen. Keep your promise.

🖐 Respect the goals and objectives of the meeting by listening and responding sincerely.

🖐 Ask more open-ended questions than close-ended ones.

🖐 Pause for five seconds before answering difficult questions. These pauses allow you to formulate well-thought-out answers. Remember that silence is the most effective tool of empathic communicators.

🖐 Ask for a second meeting; this will allow you to collect more information, if necessary. If the other party has any documents that may be of use to you, be sure to ask for copies so that you have time to review them.

🖐 Strive to end the meeting with two winners.

🖐 Summarize your understanding of the meeting and ask the other person if you understood correctly. Leave the meeting ensuring that both parties are content.

After the Meeting

After the meeting, write a postmortem analysis on the quality of your communication. Writing is the most powerful tool at your disposal to improve your new set of skills. To increase the value of this exercise, have a mentor to help you.

🖐 After the meeting, write down your impressions; analyze your best strategies so you can repeat them, as well as the worst ones so you can avoid them. This will improve your ability to listen to understand.

The Magic of Empathy

In this section, I will share with you some stories that have affected me as a mother, as a colleague, and as a doctor. I was surprised by the magical results of these conversations. In each of them, I was moved by the authenticity of emotions I experienced. I'm grateful to be sharing these experiences with you. Here are some examples of conversations, including with two examples of group communication that I call *mega communication*.

Interpersonal Communication

The following short stories illustrate how one-on-one empathic conversations can be as magical as it is powerful.

Mom, I Am Planning a Sleepover at My Friend's House

I sincerely believe that the best place to learn and practice your communication skills is at home or at the office. To illustrate my point, I have chosen to tell you about a conversation I once had with my sixteen-year-old son.

One day, he came into the kitchen and told me that he was planning a sleepover at his friend's house. I asked him for the parents' address and telephone number to make sure that a responsible person would be present. Following my request, my hormonal teenage son erupted like an angry volcano. There was absolutely no way he was going to reveal his plans to me.

Coincidentally, I had just read Steven Covey's book *The 7 Habits in Action*. This was the perfect opportunity for me to practice the "Three Lives Game," a negotiation technique suggested by the author. I calmly looked for a deck of cards, and then took three cards and gave three others to my son. I invited him to play the game. Intrigued, he agreed to listen to the instructions. "I understand that you want to go sleep at your friend's house. As for me, I want to know where you're going, and I want to talk to the parents. We'll talk calmly to find common ground. We each have three lives. If one of us screams, interrupts, or gets angry, he loses a life." At this point, my son was still listening.

I continued with the instructions: "The goal is to reach an agreement while we still have at least one card. The one who loses all three cards loses the game. If you lose all your cards, you won't go to your friend's house. If I lose all my cards, then you can leave without telling me where you are going, and without letting me talk to the parents. However, we can find a win-win solution while we still have our cards, and that solution will be the chosen one."

Much to my surprise, he accepted the challenge. It was not easy to play against a teenager. We both lost two cards. The situation was getting worse. Neither of us wanted to lose. With two cards left on the table, our game was reaching a critical peak.

I asked him how he was going to get to his friend's house. He replied that he would take the bus, and that it would take him an hour to get there. I offered to drive him and pick him up in exchange for the information I was asking for, and then I let silence work its magic.

During the pause, he probably figured out that a twenty-minute ride in a warm, comfortable car was better than waiting in the cold for a bus with the risk of missing it. He finally smiled and accepted my offer. We settled our dispute peacefully. I was able to call the parents, and I drove my son to his friend's house.

I have never forgotten this game. I did it a few more times with my son, but after a while, we no longer needed the cards to find solutions to our conflicts, which became less frequent and less intense as my son grew up.

53

This game works great with teenagers, who love challenges. But be careful: teenagers will push you to your limits and may do anything to make you lose your cards. Keep in mind that it may be unprofessional to bring a deck of cards to negotiate with your boss or business partners.

Mom, I Don't Want to Go to the Restaurant

When my two boys were eight and ten years old, we took them to Walt Disney World. To have them understand the cost of the trip, they had to help us in choosing the hotels, activities, and restaurants. The instructions were made clear from the beginning. The travel budget had to be respected. We gave each child a certain amount to spend on souvenirs, and they had to use it throughout the two-week trip. We thought it would be a good life lesson for them.

Everything went exactly as planned. The children didn't plead for extra activities or more gifts. One night near the end of our trip, I got tired, and I said to my husband, "Let's go to the restaurant for some pizza."

My son immediately started crying. He would not stop crying. He didn't want to go to a restaurant for dinner. I didn't understand; pizza was one of his favorite foods! Through many, many tears, my son told us that if we were to go out for pizza, we would exceed our budget. He said that he was afraid to descend into poverty and not have any more money. In the end, we decided to forego the pizza and eat dinner at the hotel instead, as we had originally planned.

> My son's woeful misunderstanding of budgets
> illustrates the power that our words have over others.
> The power of our words is all the more magnified
> when we are speaking as an authority figure. Children,
> as well as employees, are sensitive to the expectations
> of their parents and bosses.

Doctor, I Don't Want to Go Home

A medical student told me one day, while doing a vascular surgery internship in an English-speaking hospital in Montreal, that she was caring for an elderly woman who was having trouble speaking English. On the day the patient was to be discharged, she categorically refused to leave. The medical team agreed to let her stay for one more day. The next day, she was even more strongly opposed to being discharged. Without really understanding, the doctors agreed to keep her. This lasted for a week.

The medical student, inexperienced and armed only with the information provided by her medical textbooks, mustered all of her courage and paid a visit to this increasingly difficult patient. After a few minutes, she left the room and promptly told the nurses that the patient would be leaving later that afternoon. When the medical team met later that day, her supervisor asked how she had managed to placate the patient. She replied that she had simply asked the patient, "Why are you refusing to leave?"

The patient candidly replied, "I am afraid of falling down the stairs because I live on the second floor, and there are no elevators."

The student then offered her physiotherapy and home nursing services to help her regain her mobility and confidence. The patient agreed to go back home.

In this story, the young medical student demonstrated the power of empathic communication by working with the patient to understand her fears and find a solution. It is a shame that the patient had to stay in the hospital for a week longer than necessary.

A Vile Viremia

On Mother's Day eve, a mother and her daughter walked into the clinic without an appointment. The little girl had a tiny pimple on her thigh. The anxious mother asked if her daughter was contagious. I quickly replied and assured her that her daughter was not contagious. Despite this, the mother's agitation increased, and I remained silent, not knowing how to tell this mother her daughter simply had a mosquito bite.

She persisted. "Doctor, I am sure that my daughter is contagious! We have a family party tomorrow, she's going to get the other children sick." At that moment, I understood that this mother was looking for a reason to be absent from the Mother's Day party the following day. As she was not able to find another excuse, I gave her one.

"You can tell your family," I replied, "that the doctor told you that your child has a nasty contagious viremia. It will be my fault and not yours if you do not show up." Upon saying these words, we both burst out laughing.

Brief interactions like these illustrate how important it is to understand someone else's distress and motivation. Opportunities to practice empathy arise in all circumstances. I'm sure this mother used my excuse and was able to justify her absence.

I Don't Want to Go to My Father's House

One day, a friend of mine, a lawyer, asked me to evaluate a three-year-old child who was refusing to go to his father's house following his parents' divorce. Both parents were well respected in their professional fields. Neither of them was abusing alcohol or drugs. There was no history of domestic violence. Several experts had determined that both parents were fit to parent their child. Yet, the child categorically refused to go to his father's house.

After spending thousands of dollars on parenting experts and therapies, my friend the lawyer suggested to the parents that they come to see me, as I had extensive experience with children.

I arranged for a meeting to be held in the presence of both parents and the child. After ensuring that everyone was comfortable, I explored an often-forgotten angle in the assessment of children experiencing their parents' divorce. I wanted to know if the child felt any guilt about the separation. This was not the case.

An hour later, I had still not found the cause of the child's distress. I asked him, "If you were to spend two days at your father's house, what would happen?" He immediately replied, "I would starve to death."

58

No one expected this heartfelt answer. I asked him why he would starve to death. He told me that since his dad didn't cook, staying at his house would surely result in starvation. He had never seen his father cook. This child was absolutely convinced that spending time with his dad would result in his death.

Later that evening, the father went to his ex-wife's house and made an omelet for his son. From that day on, the child agreed to go to his father's house without hesitation.

This kind of story can only happen to children who might not have all the necessary information to make the right decisions. At this age, they cannot analyze with discernment as adults do. They instinctively act to ensure their own survival by making decisions based on their limited understanding of the world.

This example illustrates the importance of identifying
the reasons behind those who seek to protect
themselves when there is no apparent danger.
Only open-ended questions can help solve
these mysteries, especially when dealing with children
in distress who need to be comforted and freed
from any feelings of guilt.

Doctor! My Ankle Hurts

One evening, when I was on call in the emergency room, 59
I saw a young woman who had a sore ankle. Tears were
pouring from her face, and she was clearly in distress.

After examining her ankle and analyzing the X-rays, I
told her that she was suffering from a sprain. I gave her
a prescription for pain relievers and a two-week sick
note. The poor woman burst into tears again and became
inconsolable.

I thought it was good news that she didn't have a fracture
and only needed a little rest to get her back on her feet. I
resolved to find the cause of her distress. When I asked
what was causing her grief, she replied that she had been
studying for an entire year to become a flight attendant.
Her final exam was scheduled for the following day. She
needed to be in good shape to pass the practical tests.

If she took a two-week break, she would have to wait until the next exam period to pass her practical exam. I offered to apply a rigid bandage to her ankle and prescribed a stronger painkiller to be taken one hour before the examination. To make sure that everything went well, I scheduled a follow-up appointment two days later, after her exam.

Two days later, the young woman came back to see me. Smiling, she confirmed that she had performed very well on her exam. I reexamined her ankle and reapplied the bandage. Before leaving, she promised to take two weeks off to allow her injury to heal completely.

This case once again illustrates the power of empathic communication. An open-ended question helped uncover the mystery of this patient's grief. Unfortunately, it is not always possible to come up with a win-win solution. Indeed, if the young woman had had a fracture, she would have needed a cast. She would have been forced to wait a year before seeing her dreams come true.

Maria Goretti

One of the most unusual cases of my career was when I was working as a young doctor in northern Quebec. I had agreed care for the psychiatric patients. At that time, expert psychiatrists came to visit us at the hospital once every three weeks. In the meantime, two family doctors were in charge of the fifty beds, all consultations, and emergencies.

That day, I had a consultation to see a patient who had burned his hands during a fire at his apartment. So far, everything seemed normal. However, when he wrote his name on the meal selection sheet, he signed "Maria Goretti." Surprised, the nurses asked him for an explanation. He persisted and insisted that his name was Maria Goretti. The family doctor in charge of the case bandaged his wounds and asked for a psychiatric evaluation, as the police suspected this patient was guilty of arson.

Before I met the patient, I did a little research and discovered that he had been using this name for a very long time. For example, he signed his welfare payment checks with this fake name. Family members told me that their whole village had abandoned the idea of calling him anything other than "Maria Goretti." The patient confirmed all my suspicions and told me that he wished to be called by his chosen name. I decided to keep him under observation until he could see the psychiatrist, who would help me handle this case of psychosis.

The psychiatrist first met him without reading his file and without asking me for my opinion. When we discussed the case, the psychiatrist told me that I could discharge the patient who, in his opinion, had no psychiatric conditions. I was surprised, and we went back to see the patient together. The psychiatrist said to him, "Dr. Audet told me that you know a woman named Maria Goretti. Would you mind telling me about that?" And there was Maria Goretti again; the patient renewed his delusions for more than thirty minutes. The psychiatrist ordered Maria Goretti's hospitalization and an in-depth psychiatric evaluation.

This extreme case illustrates that some pathologies can be hidden behind completely normal-looking behaviors. This type of encapsulated psychosis is not always easy to identify.

My Beloved Autistic Children

During my first year of practice in a remote area, I chose to devote the majority of my time caring for children. I thought I could be a good influence and help them grow. A doctor who was leaving his post offered me a position caring for autistic children living in a specialized center.

During my first visit, I was shocked by my surroundings. New toys were stacked in the middle of a large playroom, isolated and untouched. The toys, just like the children, seemed to suffer from neglect. Luc, six years old, the youngest resident, was staring at a beautifully decorated wall. Another child seemed hypnotized by the circular movement of a spinning top. Yet another was clapping his hands for no apparent reason.

The nurse explained to me that the majority of the residents completely refused to communicate. They had to wear diapers and were often aggressive with each other or with the staff. Unable to cope with their aggressiveness, the educators were forced to make them wear hockey helmets and sometimes boxing gloves to prevent them from hurting themselves. To make matters worse, the nurse informed me that the majority of parents no longer visited their children; only a few of them sent a gift on Christmas or on their child's birthday. The luckiest, often the least ill, would go out for a few hours each month for a family meal.

63

There was nothing I had learned in medical school that could have prepared me this. I knew of no treatment for these children. How could I make them understand that I was trying to help them? My friends had warned me that this task would be an insurmountable one. I was discouraged after this initial visit, and I needed to take my mind off things. Later that evening, I watched a movie. The main character was a psychiatric hospital doctor. The majority of his patients couldn't return home or hold a job. Surprisingly, they all seemed calm. No patient wore a straitjacket. Educators and patients were laughing in the courtyard or playing with a ball.

Later in the film, a journalist asked the doctor about the secret of his success. He replied that when he first arrived, all the patients were living in isolation. Most of them were wearing physical restraints. He said that as a team, they had trained the patients one by one, one minute at a time. They had even introduced the patients to arts and music. According to him, the most important thing was to believe in their success. He concluded by saying that this unusual practice had enhanced the lives of the entire staff as well. By the end of the movie, I was resolved to try this method with my new patients.

For more than a year, the educators were committed to engaging with the kids one at a time. We had them listen to music, introduced them to relaxation techniques, and allowed them to draw with their fingers. Sometimes they would smile back at us, and sometimes they wouldn't. It took a while, but the whole team was optimistic about our progress.

When summer came, the children had a great time at the summer camp we had organized for them by the lake. Together we celebrated the handing over of the helmets and boxing gloves that had become useless. No one came to pick the children up, and they would not be going to school, but they were finally opening up. These autistic children influenced all of us in ways we never could have imagined. We all grew into better people as a result of this experience.

64

I thank these children for allowing me to develop communication strategies that are different from those generally used. Autistic people have sensory hypersensitivity that requires proper training and patience to overcome.

Nowadays, we have special needs classes for children on the spectrum. Fortunately, there has been progress in neuropsychology, which has opened up different and effective channels of communication with the vast majority of children diagnosed with pervasive developmental disorders that we once called autism.

65

When There Are No Words

I was on call in the emergency room one Christmas night. The emergency room triage nurse triggered the "Pink Code" for a newborn in distress. Not knowing anything about the circumstances surrounding the cardiorespiratory arrest, the on-call team I was leading tried to resuscitate the little boy in the hopes of saving him. We were worried about his heart. It would start beating, stop, and start again. We were worried about his blue lips too. I was hopeful yet felt powerless in my attempts to resuscitate him, but I steeled my resolve and kept trying.

The nurses and my colleagues were waiting for my instructions. I was thinking of my own children, waiting for me at home to open their presents. I could hear the parents crying in the waiting room. First, a nurse put her hand on my shoulder and then whispered the child's story in my ear. He had been born prematurely three weeks earlier. He had stopped breathing at home, and no assistance was given during the 20-minute drive to the hospital. She explained that the parents had two young daughters and that the child was their only son.

I was deeply moved. It reminded me of my three miscarriages and my two boys, who came later. This new knowledge forced me to make a difficult decision. By relentlessly trying to save him, I was condemning him to a life in a permanently vegetative state. After 45 minutes of trying, I whispered, "Let's stop the resuscitation procedures." His little heartbeats slowly stopped. The rhythmic sound of the monitor going "beep, beep" slowly morphed into silence, signaling the end. Everyone looked down as I pronounced the death.

The hardest part was yet to come; I had to meet his parents. I couldn't find the words to announce this terrible tragedy. I walked up to the room where they were waiting for me. When I walked in, I looked at the mother. Our mothers' hearts understood each other. I opened my arms to embrace her, and we cried together for about ten minutes without talking. I couldn't think of a single word to describe how I was feeling.

Then I stepped back into my role as a caregiver. Despite the pain, I had to pull myself together. I had to announce that an autopsy was needed. Once this task was completed, I was able to offer my assistance to the grieving parents.

That night, I arrived home very late. My children and my husband had fallen asleep in the living room. They hadn't opened their presents. I sat near the Christmas tree and sobbed softly, thinking about how lucky I was to be a mother and about the demanding responsibilities of being a family doctor.

Thirty years later, my husband's daughter lost her battle against cancer. Sylvain and I were both present to witness her last breath. My colleagues, parents, and friends tried in vain to find the right words to comfort me, as I had so often tried to do for others in the course of my career. The French singer Lynda Lemay solved the mystery. In her song "Pas de mot" ("No Words"), she said that no scribe nor English language expert has ever found the right word to describe the feelings of parents who lose one of their children. Lemay poetically comes to the conclusion that there are no words in our dictionaries to name the pain of parents who go through their child's accidental or inevitable death.

67

In life, there are times when there are no words to communicate our empathy. A pat on the shoulder and a hug are more meaningful than any words when comforting your bereaved loved ones.

Group Communication

We have seen how empathy can be powerful and magical in one-on-one conversations. The magic of empathy is also possible when we address a larger audience, such as during a workshop, a keynote speech, a lecture, or when managing a crisis, as shown in the two following stories.

Commander in Spite of Myself

During one of my first on-call days at the Rouyn-Noranda emergency unit, I received a call from the director of public safety, saying, "Dr. Audet, an explosion has just occurred at the airport's waiting room. According to the protocol, you must initiate and supervise the "Red Code" while maintaining emergency services. The number of those seriously injured is estimated to be twelve. More than forty people are suffering from minor trauma or nervous shock. Ambulance attendants, firefighters, and police officers are on their way to the hospital."

After assuring him of my cooperation, I dropped the handset. My fast heart rate, the sweat on my palms, and the speed of my thoughts all shared a common cause. I was in a state of panic. Although I had just taken the crisis intervention courses and had studied all the protocols that had to be followed, I had wished would never have to go through such an experience.

I was wondering if my three months of experience would be enough for me to make the right decisions and manage all the staff, who were much more experienced than I was. My inner voice was screaming, "If you make a mistake, everyone will think you're a bad doctor."

The head nurse asked me, "Doctor, can I be of any help?"

"Initiate the Red Code," I replied. "All the doctors, nurses, and managers have to come to help us. If a serious case arrives, set it up in the resuscitation room and notify me." Without waiting for her response, I ran toward the entrance hall to organize the triage. I heard the general call, "Red Code at the ER! Red Code at the ER! Red Code at the ER!"

In less than three minutes, the attendants lined up stretchers. The staff was waiting for my instructions. When I saw Dr. Carter, the dean of the hospital, running up the stairs to the main entrance, I thought I could ask him to take my place. He put an end to my plan by asking me, "What should I do?"

Without hesitation, I gave him an order, "Sort the patients in the center of the lobby. The corridor on the right will serve as a temporary morgue. You will use the one on the left for the treatment of minor injuries. Victims with severe injuries will go directly to the operating room."

In the meantime, surgeons and anesthetists came up to me. I pointed my finger at the second floor. "Go upstairs and get the operating rooms ready. The first victims are about to arrive." Then I said to the managers, "Set up a press room. Open the auditorium for the families. Order coffee and food."

At the same time, the head nurse of the emergency room came up to me, "Doctor, a cardiac patient has just arrived at the emergency room. I think it might be a heart attack. I set him up in the resuscitation room."

Despite my fears, I had to delegate—and quickly. I summoned my colleague. "Dr. Wilson! Go right away to the resuscitation room. It's an emergency." Much to my amazement, this gray-haired doctor obeyed and did so.

The sounds of sirens from several ambulances brought me back to reality. Stretchers were parading through the improvised triage area. A dozen injured, mostly young people, were shouting, crying in agony. I could barely concentrate amid the chaos. Two boys had open fractures on their legs. Their scarlet blankets reflected the severity of their bleeding. Another one was holding his shredded hand, which was covered with a blood-soaked bandage. Three unconscious victims were experiencing respiratory distress. As planned, Dr. Carter directed them to the operating room.

70

Taking advantage of the temporary lull, a journalist, a photographer, and a cameraman stood in front of me. The journalist fired several questions in a row. "Doctor, how many people were injured or killed? Was it a bomb that caused the explosion? Who is claiming responsibility for this terrorist attack?"

I could only see his big microphone in front of my face. My heart was threatening to burst through my chest. My legs were crumbling under the pressure of this tragedy. Trying to stay calm, I replied, "Our medical team and public safety have the situation under control. At the moment, I have about a dozen people injured. There are no deaths. You should understand that I can't reveal the identities of the victims until I have notified their relatives. I'll come back to give you a report in two hours." With these words, the journalist left with his team. They interviewed the injured people brought in by the Red Cross bus.

This respite lasted only a moment. Men, women, and children were rushing up and down the stairs, screaming. They were running all over the place. Notified by the media, all these people arrived to check on their loved ones. In the procedures manual, I had read that the manager of the hospital, social workers, and psychologists had to meet with the families in the auditorium; no instructions explained how to handle a hundred hysterical people. I had to improvise again.

People were grabbing my hand. They were begging me, "Is William Delves hurt? Where is Steve Biden? My son's name is David. I want to see him now." While social workers and psychologists escorted families into the auditorium, my neighbor came running in. She grabbed my shoulders and cried, "Where is Max?" I couldn't find the words to tell her that her son was in the operating room. I was wondering how to comfort her without giving her false hope. In silence, I laid my hands on hers. We made eye contact. Crying with her was not the right thing to do. I could barely believe it myself. When I said, "Don't worry, everything will be fine. We have the situation under control."

As I uttered these words, the journalist came back to me. "Doctor, how is the situation developing?" Before I had the chance to reply, the director of public health took his microphone and announced, "The Red Code simulation is over. Thank you for your participation. Tomorrow, we will assess in detail the application of the protocol."

As soon as these words were spoken, the actors, the army cadets, removed their bandages and jumped off their stretchers. Those who played the role of desperate parents stopped screaming and crying. The photographer captured the scene. The journalist interviewed the young participants. A teenager wearing makeup told him that he'd had a "Super cool" Saturday evening.

The head nurse of the emergency room came back for me, "Doctor, come quickly, the real patient is not well. His pain is increasing. Dr. Wilson had to leave the resuscitation room to go to the delivery room."

As I ran to the emergency room, I couldn't convince myself that everything was only a simulation. For me, the stakes were quite real. I was actually being tested. The final report would contain a detailed analysis of my decisions. I was panicked at the thought of not having been up to the task so early in my career.

The next day, the director of public health came to see me and asked, "Doctor, how did you manage to stay so calm? You were amazing!"

I replied, keeping my sweaty hands in my pockets, "I simply followed the protocol. For me, it was not a game."

Fortunately, during my career, I had only one experience like this one. If this ever happens to you, delegate tasks, stay calm, manage your emotions, and communicate with the appropriate authorities and all those involved in the crisis. But believe me, nothing can prepare you for this kind of unexpected situation, even an excellent simulation. Here again, empathy is the best tool to manage any crisis.

Speech on the Power of Communication

In June 2018, my literary agent, Danielle Hampson, who lives in Arizona, asked if I would be willing to give the keynote speech at the 10th Symposium of the Academy for the Future of Women at Sias University in China. Without any hesitation, I accepted this challenge of speaking in front of nearly five thousand attendees in a foreign country.

Before going any further, let me set the context of this request. Sias University in China was founded in 1998. It is the only American University in central China. Fort Hays University in Kansas supports this institution, which is attended by nearly 30,000 students who can study English and receive an American and Chinese degree.

Ten years ago, Jerrie Ueberle created the Academy for the Future of Women in Phoenix, Arizona. For the past 10 years, this academy, which hosts about a hundred students from Sias University, has been organizing an annual leadership congress on the theme of the future of women.

73

My agent has been working with Mrs. Ueberle for several years. One of her tasks was to organize the annual Symposium. She had to find two keynote speakers and workshop leaders; hence, my invitation to give an opening speech and to lead a workshop. I had chosen the theme of the power of heart-to-heart empathic communication. I was very excited about going to China. I had even studied Chinese for almost six months to be able to communicate with the students.

Unfortunately, a few months later, the trade relationship between the Chinese, Americans, and Canadians deteriorated, and I had to cancel my trip. I chose to see this obstacle as an opportunity to publish my speech in this book.

The Power of Listening

Like most of you, when obstacles arose in the pursuit of my dreams, I thought of giving up everything. My dream was to become a published author. A few years ago, despite good sales and many international literary awards, I was accumulating mistakes, failures, and rejections. I thought of giving up.

Then, one day, I had the chance to meet Danielle Hampson, who took the time to listen to me. Much to my surprise, she wanted to know everything about the family doctor who wrote educational books for children. I immediately felt her sincere desire to listen to me, help me, and guide me. I felt comfortable, and I wanted to talk to her about myself with complete sincerity.

I explained to her that after reading a book written by a doctor and writer, I had decided to follow his path, without realizing how difficult these two professions were. After listening to me, Danielle offered to become my agent for the promotion of my educational series, Felix and Booboo. She was convinced of the series' potential. Her trust and empathic listening helped me to regain confidence and to not give up. So I took back control of my passion, my confidence, and I was ready to continue.

Today, more than ever, I intend to devote my life to changing the world, one young reader at a time. I mean, can you imagine? Without my friend and agent Danielle, my publishing house would have burnt my unsold books, as they had decided to stop distributing them.

I wanted to start my speech with this story to illustrate the power of heart-to-heart communication, which is often initiated by an empathetic listener. Without Danielle's help, my work would have fallen into disuse, and I would not be standing before you this morning. A single conversation allowed me to regain control of the pursuit of my dream. What an impact! I mean, that's magic!

I will share with you two other stories that illustrate the power of empathic communication; both are experiences I had in the course of my career as a doctor and teacher.

FIRST STORY: **Amy's Tears**

On the day of my first night on-call shifts at the hospital, as a young student, I was called around midnight to attend to little Amy, who was crying. She had to have one of her eyes removed due to severe trauma.

Surgeons had to quickly remove the traumatized eye to prevent her own antibodies from attacking both eyes, which would render her completely blind. The operation was scheduled for the following morning.

I didn't know how to deal with her distress. I was just a medical student. I had just memorized tons of medical books, but no one had ever taught me how to comfort a sad and frightened little girl. She answered "No" to my three medical questions. She knew she'd be asleep. She understood that she would have an eye prosthesis. She knew she wouldn't go blind.

After these close-ended questions, I changed my strategy and asked an open-ended question, "Amy, why are you crying?" This open-ended question allowed me to uncover Amy's secret. I was shocked when she told me that she wanted to enjoy the last time she could cry. She thought that after the surgery, she wouldn't be able to cry anymore.

To comfort her, I drew a picture of the tear sac located under her eye, explaining that the surgeon would not remove it. After promising her that she could cry again for the rest of her life, she smiled at me and fell into a deep sleep, appeased.

I have never forgotten this first contact with a patient. Several years later, as a medical teacher, I told this story to my students to demonstrate the importance of empathic listening in caring for their patients. This competency is an essential element in the toolkits of all physicians, all nurses, and all leaders in their respective fields.

SECOND STORY: Judy's Success

When I first met Judy, she was completing her family medicine residency. In less than six months, she would be a family doctor. Unfortunately, all the professors agreed that she would most likely fail unless a miracle happened.

That month, I was in charge of assessing her ability to question a patient in the psychiatry department by observing her behind a hidden mirror. The first time I saw Judy interviewing a patient, I understood her problem. She wasn't a good listener! Judy was always asking questions. She wouldn't wait for the answers before continuing. She seemed afraid of the silence!

The next day, I invited her to my office an hour before the opening of the clinic. While enjoying a cup of coffee, I asked her to tell me about her most beautiful childhood memory. I waited for her answer in silence while she was busy thinking.

She smiled and told me she had liked fishing with her father on a beautiful lake. I asked her to close her eyes and go back to the boat in her mind with her father. After a second short pause, I asked if she was rowing, if she heard any noise, or if she was moving in the boat. She answered "No" to all my questions because to catch fish, you had to stay still and in silence.

Then I explained to her that medicine was like going fishing. If the doctor remained silent after each open-ended question, he might catch a fish, or discover his patient's secrets. Each of our questions had the power to catch a fish or discover the patient's secret if the doctor kept quiet after each open-ended question.

Silence has the power to allow the patient to formulate their response. Patients feel more comfortable sharing their secrets when their listeners pause and stay remain silent, I told Judy to meditate before seeing the next patient and to focus on the patient's needs. I told her to use this simple technique: pause for five seconds after asking a question to let the patient think before answering.

That day, Judy conducted an excellent patient interview. She used my technique, and made the right diagnosis and negotiated a treatment plan with her patient. She was proud of herself.

Six months later, Judy told me that before her final exams, she closed her eyes. She went back to her father's boat to fish. These few minutes of meditation calmed her down and allowed her to pass her exam with honors.

Do you want to become an empathic communicator, like Judy? If so, then you must learn to overcome your fear of silence. Silence and active listening go hand in hand. These stories each illustrate, in their own way, the power and magic of empathic communication and its best ally: silence.

You may be wondering when the best time is to practice empathic communication. The answer is simple: everywhere and all the time! Leaders have a responsibility to recognize these moments, and to seize the opportunity to listen to an individual in need, even if it is someone you don't particularly like. If you want to make a difference in your field, take every opportunity to exert your positive influence on others.

You are here to become the leaders of tomorrow. Like my young medical students, you all want to change the world. I admire your motivation to commit yourself to achieve at least one of the United Nations' seventeen sustainable development goals.

It won't be easy. You will need a good dose of perseverance, patience, and passion. There will be several obstacles. That is a guarantee. But never give up.

As a doctor and leader, I have chosen one of these objectives. My dream is to make children love to read and to help improve their level of literacy. To achieve it, I used to collaborate with charity to give copies of my books to poor children.

Now, I write stories to promote the language development, reading, and critical thinking of young readers. I know that when children read or are read a story, it develops their value system, expands their imagination, and improves their ability to solve problems. This is their first step toward freedom of thought.

I must emphasize a very important lesson from my first story. As tomorrow's leaders, make a promise to yourselves to resist the temptation to become isolated in times of vulnerability. There's always a friend ready to listen to you. Surround yourself with mentors who listen to your problems and needs, and speak from your heart. Women and men of honor feed off of their relationships with competent mentors, who help them bounce back after failures.

Dear future leaders, you now know two keys to your success: speaking to be understood, and listening to understand. The secret lies in true heart-to-heart communication.

Keep in mind that the time spent listening to your friends, your enemies, or children will prove more valuable than the words you say to them. On the other hand, if you feel sad, lonely, or angry, do not hesitate to confide in an experienced mentor.

In conclusion, remember Zeno of Citium, a Greek philosopher, who said, "You have two ears and a mouth, so listen twice as often as you speak." To do this, especially before a complex conversation, clear your head for five seconds and focus on your task: empathic listening.

Ask open-ended questions to understand the other person's emotions, without judging or giving advice. Let silence do its work and wait for the results. Be prepared to be a confidant to those around you and exercise your leadership, just as I have done as a doctor and medical professor in my country, Canada.

Thank you for listening, and good luck in your lives as leaders!

Conclusion

realized that the most beautiful moments of my life or career were those in which I communicated honestly with the people around me. These beautiful exchanges have reached depths that can only be achieved through empathy. These were truly magical moments in my life.

As I pointed out at the beginning of this book, I was captivated by the technology that has invaded our lives, to the point of isolating myself. Technology has changed all of our lives. It was and must remain an excellent servant, but I must strive to not let the new technology, with its various means of communication, become my master.

If I had to summarize my book in a single sentence, here is what I would write:

EMPATHIC COMMUNICATION REQUIRES
PREPARATION, CONCENTRATION, AND
A WILLINGNESS TO OPEN UP TO OTHERS BUT ITS
BENEFITS ARE BEYOND ALL EXPECTATIONS
FOR THOSE WHO PRACTICE
AND MASTER IT.

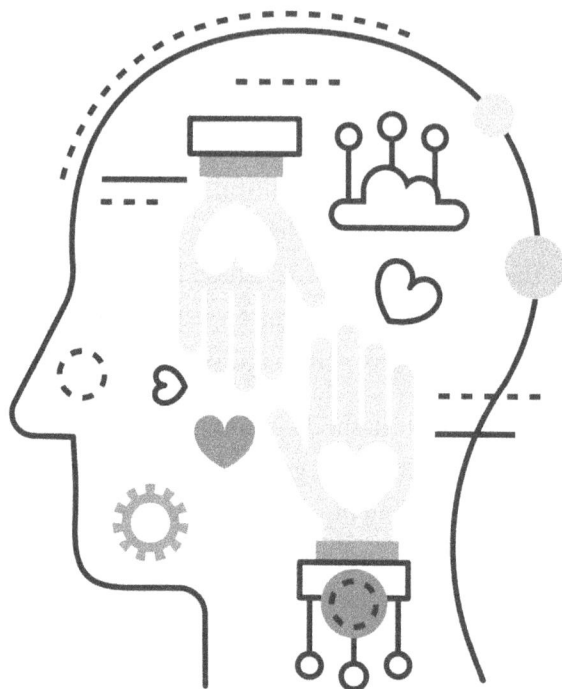

Take the time to write your
communication logbook.

Writing Is a Therapeutic Tool

In the next few pages, I encourage you to keep a journal of your empathetic communications with your children, your boss, your colleagues, or your business partners. There are many opportunities for you to practice. The more you practice, the better you will become.

Be as specific as possible. Feel free to review these pages on a regular basis. You will be surprised by your progress.

Follow this step-by-step guide.

Perceiving Emotions

Over the next few days, try to perceive the emotions of your interlocutors. Take time to note these emotions. Perceiving emotions is the first skill to acquire.

> Example 1: My teenager is screaming at me. He hits the table with his fists and runs to his room, slamming the door.
>
> Example 2: Your boss seems to be worried. She doesn't talk much and stays in her office. She holds her head in her hands. She seems scared.

What emotions do you perceive in these examples?

_____

_____

_____

_____

_____

_____

Interpreting Non-Verbal Language

Once you are better at detecting emotions, try to interpret the non-verbal language of your interlocutors. Note these emotions and the verbal and non-verbal signs. Body language tells a lot about the emotions driving people's behavior and decisions. Take the time to record your observations.

84

What non-verbal language do you perceive during your communication?

_____

_____

_____

_____

_____

Your Empathic Conversations

Once you are better at perceiving emotions and non-verbal language, practice initiating empathetic conversations. Write down your experiences, and then analyze them to improve yourself. Analyze how it was difficult to achieve your goals.

What empathic communications have you had?

_____

_____

_____

_____

_____

_____

What obstacles did you face?

_____

_____

_____

_____

_____

_____

Note how your new skills improve the quality of your communications. What is the impact of your new skills on yourself? On others?

_____

_____

_____

_____

_____

_____

_____

_____

References

Here is a list of books that have helped me to improve my communication skills. As several publishing houses produced them, I decided to provide book titles and their authors. They are available in hard copy, digital formats, and some as audiobooks.

Dale Carnegie
- *How to Win Friends and Influence People*

This classic book on communication and interpersonal relationships is worth reading and rereading. Filled with simple and well-chosen examples, it will have a significant impact on your life.

I also suggest *How to Stop Worrying and Start Living,* by the same author.

There are communication and leadership courses sponsored by the Dale Carnegie International Organization. The basic course lasts for forty-five hours and is offered three hours per week.

Stephen Covey
- *The 7 Habits of Highly Effective People*
- *First Things First*
- *The 7 Habits in Action*

The first book presents a theoretical framework of the seven habits of highly effective people. The second helps readers to set priorities in their life. In his third book, the author tells and analyzes stories where each of the habits is applied to a specific situation. I found these books very inspiring. I have read them many times.

Michael Balint

- *The Doctor, His Patient, and the Illness*

This wonderful book illustrates all the concepts of empathic communication that I present in this book written for health professionals.

Thomas d'Asembourg

- *Being Genuine: Stop Being Nice, Start Being Real*

This book helps readers to recognize their tendency to ignore their own needs and to pass their frustration on to others, thereby creating a vicious circle of misunderstanding. The reader will learn to recognize their needs and to put them to the service of authentic and enriching communication. Everyone should read this book.

Colette Portelance

- *Authentic Communication:*
  In Praise of Intimate Relationships

In this book, the author invites the reader to gently open up the doors of intimacy between people who care about each other. You will discover levels of communication, barriers, and facilitators that enhance authentic communication. You will certainly like the other books of this prolific author, who specializes in helping people with their relationships.

John Gray

- *Men Are from Mars, Women Are from Venus*

I laughed so much as I read this tale on men and women's relationships. In this book, the author concluded that men focus on competence and handle stress by becoming silent and hiding in their cave. On the other hand, women focus on the quality of relationships and want to be heard when they face a problem. However, both look to solve their problems by themselves. Obviously, there are some nuances, but knowing these differences helps you get ready for empathic communication as a couple.

Stephen Trzeciak and Anthony Mazzarelli

- *Compassionomics: The Revolutionary Scientific Evidence that Caring Makes a Difference*

Well-researched, well written and comprehensive, this book lists all the evidences of the power of kindness health care. Every health professionals and students should read this book and practice compassion. As proven by many studies, it improves quality of care, patients' compliance and reduce caregivers' risk of burnout.

One of the best books I ever read on patient and their caregivers' relationships.

89

Logbook of Your Empathic Communications

91

Bibliography

Recent books published in hard copy, digitally, and/or as audiobooks:

SÉRIE FÉLIX ET BOUBOU/FELIX AND BOOBOO SERIES
2017/Les éditions Dre Nicole

- Des biscuits pour Gabriel (Allergies)
- Léa a mal au cœur (Gastro-entérite)
- Charles s'est blessé en jouant (Bras cassé)
- Félix au musée du corps humain (Corps humain)
- Joëlle va chez le docteur (Vaccination)
- Joëlle se gratte la tête (Poux)
- Lucas a mal aux oreilles (Otites)
- Sabrina a des boutons (Varicelle)

2017/Dr. Nicole Publishing

- Special Food for Sam (Allergies)
- Lea Does Not Feel Well (Gastroenteritis)
- Charles Hurt Himself Playing (Broken Arm)
- Felix Is Curious about His Body (Human Body)
- Maya Visits Her Doctor (Vaccination),
- Maya's Head Is Itching (Lice)
- Lucas Has an Earache (Otitis)
- Amy Has a Rash (Chickenpox)

2017 **PARENTS FOR SALE,** Coloring Book, Dr. Nicole Publishing

2016 **PARENTS FOR SALE,** Audiobook RavenPheat Production

2015 **PARENTS FOR SALE,** AuthorHouse

2015 **VENTE DE PARENTS,** Boomerang

2015 **ARE YOU EATING MY LUNCH?/MANGES-TU MON LUNCH?** AuthorHouse

2015 **STRIKE AT CHARLES'S FARM/GRÈVE À LA FERME DE CHARLES,** AuthorHouse

2012 **VOTRE GUIDE SANTÉ INFO,** Guy Saint-Jean editor

Literary Awards

- Classic Literary Award
- Mom's Choice Award
- Readers' Favorite Gold and Bronze Medal
- Story Monster Approved
- 50 Great Writers You Should Be Reading
- Top Female Children's Book Author

95

For a complete list of the author's publications and awards, visit her website: DrNicoleBook.com

Conferences

Dr. Nicole is a professional speaker and personal coach. She gives workshops, keynote speeches, and lectures to parents, teachers, health professionals, authors, and managers. She is available for book signing.

Below are samples of workshop topics:

- The International Book Market
- The Pros and Cons of Self-Publishing
- The Development of Children from Zero to Nine Years Old
- The Art of Public Speaking
- Empathic Communication

Dr. Nicole Publishing can customize her books for companies who wish to offer them to their employees or charities. It is possible to add the company's logo on the cover page and a page written by the President.

Contact

- Email: nicole@nicoleaudet.com
- Websites: DrNicoleBook.com / FelixandBooboo.com

www.ingramcontent.com/pod-product-compliance
Lightning Source LLC
Chambersburg PA
CBHW071139280326

41935CB00010B/1291